BILL WARD'S

GARDENING COLLECTION

DIRTY SECRETS

First Published 1999 by
Hyndman Publishing
PO Box 5017, Dunedin
ISBN 1-877168-32-7

TEXT:
© Bill Ward

CONCEPT & FORMAT:
Neil Hyndman

LAYOUT & DESIGN:
Dileva Design

PHOTOGRAPHY:
Dennis Greville

ILLUSTRATIONS:
Sheila Boerkamp

PRINTING:
Tablet Colour Print

Introduction

According to the latest Hillary Commission Report gardening in all its forms is the most popular leisure time activity in New Zealand. Many of us are challenged by the complexities of the plant kingdom. Changing lifestyles and constant time restraints mean most gardeners today are looking for simple solutions to the host of problems which prevent our plants from looking like a million dollars throughout their life cycle.

The diverse and exciting range of plants accessible to gardeners allows us to capture nature's beauty and enjoy its foliage, flowers and fruits.

The purpose of this book is to dispel some of the myths associated with gardening and to make this leisure activity as enjoyable and cost effective as it can be.

I have included practical gardening advice and some tried and true home remedies so you can understand and combat the problems and setbacks we all experience.

Cheers, and happy gardening.

Bill Ward

Thanks to the staff of Business Coaching New Zealand, especially Ruth and Mark for their ongoing support and encouragement. A special thanks also to Margaret for her time and energy in editing this book. Thanks also to Peg from Greens Garden Centre in Hamilton for her innovative ideas and continued support. To my "pumpkin" – thank you for your constant support.

Contents

Secrets to Good Gardening

Take a tip from me, the secret to good gardening is simplicity. An understanding of how to achieve the look you want by using the most suitable plants for your situation will go a long way towards making gardening a relaxing and stress-free hobby.

WHAT TYPE OF GARDENER ARE YOU?

Essentially there are three types of gardener – the infrequent gardener, the once a month gardener, and, like most of us, the weekend gardener. Being an infrequent gardener doesn't mean we enjoy our gardens any less – some of the most beautiful gardens I know are those of friends who have planned their garden so it only needs occasional work. Most weekends they are entertaining in and enjoying their patch – a garden really should be a place of pleasure, not a chore.

CHOOSE THE RIGHT PLANTS FOR YOUR LOCATION AND FOR YOU

Identify the types of plants that will do well in your patch.

Some gardeners will persevere with the most difficult specimens but most of us want a garden that is relatively easy to care for and looks fabulous most of the time.

Walking around your neighbourhood will help you discover what plants do well in your area – this is also a great way to meet people, make some friends and share ideas. Don't be afraid to knock on someone's door to ask for a plant name or if you can take a cutting of a plant that catches your eye.

Plant your garden for colour, keeping in mind what works well in your locality. Most problems I encounter are from people (some landscapers included) who have planted things that appeal without regard to their suitability. Hey, a cautious approach will not stop you from being wild or a little offbeat. The plants you choose should reflect the type of gardener you are.

Secrets to Good Gardening

c o n t i n u e d

Once you have made your selection, then find the time to really understand what your plants need. Success will be yours if you treat plants like people – they need good regular feeding to be strong and healthy.

REMOVE POOR PERFORMING PLANTS

If it looks sick and does not respond to some tender care, pull it out and replace it with something else – be ruthless. If you don't your garden risks becoming nothing more than a hospital for sickly plants, leaving you disappointed and frustrated with the results.

Fertilising and feeding your plants

Timing of fertilising is crucial if the plant is to benefit.

Throughout this book I will give advice on when to fertilise and – more importantly – what type of fertiliser to use.

FERTILISERS – ORGANIC, ARTIFICIAL OR CHEMICALLY-PREPARED

Organic fertilisers can only release their nutrients when acted on by bacteria in the soil. Therefore there can be a considerable time lag between application and actual absorption by the plants.

All plants need three essential elements:
- Nitrogen to stimulate leaf growth
- Phosphorous to stimulate root growth
- Potassium to stimulate fruiting and flowering

Depending on your plant type, there's a commercial blend available which takes the hard work out of mixing your own.

Organic manures such as pig, horse, sheep, cow, cat, dog and chicken are nature's way of providing natural fertilisers – however overuse can lock up phosphates, causing stunted growth. To remedy apply 150gms of superphosphate and 100gms of ammonia sulphate – essential when using horse manure.

Chicken manure needs to be well rotted or burning of young seedlings will occur.

All natural fertilisers work best when incorporated with hay/straw or similar – you will then get the benefits of the liquid with the solid.

Liquid blood and bone and fish fertiliser are advantageous as in liquid form it is instantly available to the plant roots.

DIFFERENT FERTILISERS AND WHAT THEY DO

Dried Blood
Quick and sustained acting natural nitrogen. Use 2 dessertspoons per square metre. Liquid feeding: 1 tablespoon per 5 litres. Especially beneficial for leaf crops such as lettuce.

Fertilising and feeding your plants

c o n t i n u e d

Copper Sulphate (Bluestone)
For algae and moss on paths. Use 2 tablespoons per litre. Bordeaux Mix made as follows: dissolve 1-3 dessertspoons in about a litre of warm water. Pour this into a separate suspension of 4 dessertspoons of hydrated lime in about 3 litres of water. This is a cheap and effective fungicide. Apply in late winter to control curly leaf in stone fruit and as an inhibitor for blight on tomatoes and potatoes.

Hydrated Lime
For Bordeaux Mixture see above. To correct soil acidity use at half the rate of agricultural lime. Hydrated lime also destroys slugs and snails, but be careful not to apply around lime-intolerant plants.

Flowers of Sulphur
Combats powdery mildew and red spider. Dust plants after rain or dew. To make soil acid apply 25g per square metre.

Nitrate of Soda
Nitrogen for quick leaf growth of cabbage, lettuce, beet, corn etc. Use 1 dessertspoon per square metre.

Magnesium Sulphate (Epsom Salts)
Prompts increased plant chlorophyll production, vigour and yield in many fruiting crops, particularly tomatoes and citrus. Apply 1 handful per square metre or 100gms per tree. Liquid feeding use 20gms per 1 litre of water.

Sulphate of Iron
Controls moss in lawns – use 300gms in 10 litres of water per 10 square metres. This also acidifies, suppresses weeds and promotes healthy grass. For acid-loving plants use one handful per square metre or spray foliage with 1 teaspoon per litre. This also corrects iron deficiency in alkaline soils.

Urea
A fast acting and economical source of plant nitrogen that may be used in solid form or as a spray to give the vegetable garden a boost in early spring. Use up to 20g per square metre.

Fertilising and feeding your plants

c o n t i n u e d

Sulphate of Potash

A major nutrient for plant growth. Promotes hard, dark green, disease-resistant foliage. Improves flowering, fruit set and yield. Use 1–2 handfuls per square metre.

Sulphate of Ammonia

For vigorous lawns, or to suppress weeds, use one handful per square metre, or dissolve 300gms in 10 litres of water.
To boost growth of cabbages, lettuce and other vegetables use 30gms per square metre.

Aluminium Sulphate

Use one handful per square metre of soil two to three times a year to reduce pH for acid-loving plants such as azaleas, rhododendrons, camellias, daphne, erica, boronia etc. Deepens the blue colour in hydrangeas. Can be beneficial to ferns.

Sulphate of iron (300gms/10 litres water per 10 square metres) controls moss in lawns and suppresses weeds.

Healthy plants are what we all aspire to.

Plant troubles – why do plants die?

There are scores of problems that can account for the death of a plant – some of the most common are:

Soil and nutrition problems – Too compacted, wrong type, and/or too much food.

If too compacted the plant sits and does nothing and then slowly dies – this is common in heavy clay soils.

The wrong soil type can also kill your plants. For example, acid loving plants such as azaleas, camellias, gardenias and rhododendrons to name a few, react against too much calcium in the soil and will often collapse and die – this is common in areas such as Canterbury, Hawke's Bay and Northland.

Too much acid in the soil can also be a plant killer. Some plants such as proteas, azaleas and any others with a dense root structure that is close to the surface, can actually be killed by too much fertiliser as the roots will burn.

Watering – Over or under watering can be harmful. Water is the lifeblood of plants, but too much or too little can kill.

Sun and light – Plants have evolved over thousands of years to suit different climatic conditions – ferns love shade, cacti love sun and heat. The wrong environment for your plants can result in a disappointing performance.

Air temperature – Extreme cold, draughts, gas and fumes.

This is one area many people overlook. While most of us know frosts can kill plants, did you know gas and fumes from heating systems are also deadly to plants? Draughts are also another factor in plant death – particularly indoor plants. Bursts of cold air will shock the plant, weakening it to the point of no return.

Pests and diseases – Generally plants in poor condition are more prone to insect and fungal disease. Keep dead and dying leaves well away from your plants, as they will attract pests.

Plant troubles – common problems and what's going wrong

Plants fail for many varied reasons. To help you understand the visible signs, here are the probable effects and causes.

PLANT GROWING SLOWLY OR NOT AT ALL

Either nutritional problems or over or under watering are the possible causes. If the affected plant is in a container it may be root-bound – repotting may be the answer.

WILTING

Wilting is often the first sign of a problem – this can then be followed by leaf drop. These signs tell you the plant is under stress because of dryness, too much water or poor soil aeration.

ROTTING OF STEMS AND LEAVES

Caused by over watering of foliage during the winter months and too little warmth or sun to dry them before they are wet again.

PALE AND SPINDLY LEAVES AND GROWTH

Usually due to excess watering, under feeding and poor light. This problem is generally noticed in Spring. It can also be caused by overcrowding, which results in leggy growth.

VARIEGATED FOLIAGE TURNING GREEN

Some plants are prone to reverting to green, which is part of their physiological make-up e.g. variegated rhododendrons and hostas. Reversions in indoor plants are often due to poor light.

YELLOWING OF LEAVES AND LEAF DROP

It's perfectly normal for aged foliage to yellow and fall – however when this happens to a number of leaves the most likely reason is too much moisture, so check drainage. This can also be a root, fungal or bacteria problem.

Plant troubles – common problems and what's going wrong

c o n t i n u e d

BROWN MARGINS OR SPOTS ON LEAVES

Often due to inconsistent watering, but it is also a symptom of wet feet or the leaves being scorched by the sun. This may also be caused by over feeding.

PATTERNED YELLOWING OF LEAVES

Usually a nutritional problem or caused by insect damage – check for thrips or red spider mite.

YELLOW LEAVES WHICH REMAIN FIRM AND SMALLER THAN NORMAL

Too much lime in the compost added to lime–hating plants such as citrus – a very common problem throughout New Zealand.

PREMATURE DROPPING OF BUDS, FLOWERS, FRUIT AND LEAVES

Often due to temperature fluctuations. This can sometimes indicate a lack of moisture in the air. The two most common reasons though, are over watering or not enough water. This is a common problem for plants in containers.

WATERING TECHNIQUES

If you are concerned about over or under watering your plants then my advice is to apply a little water at first, closely monitoring the results. Over watering can kill a plant far more quickly than under watering.

Troubleshooting FUNGAL DISEASES

Problem	Diagnosis	Treatment	Natural Treatment
Botrytis (grey mould).	Occurs in damp, warm and humid conditions. Attacks leaves, stems and fruit, causing rot. Due to overcrowding and poor ventilation. Seen as greyish mould.	Thiram / saprol. Spray every 14 days where infection is evident.	Dust with flowers of sulphur. Open up infected area. Where practical remove affected material.
Citrus brown rot.	Leaves wilt and turn brown and fruit has brown rotting patches. Prevalent during late autumn and winter.	Copper oxychloride. Spray early autumn, then monthly until spring.	Garlic, chilli and onion spray. (See "Simple home-made sprays", page 63, for details.)
Downy mildew.	Wet weather disease on grapes and vegetables. Appears as small, angular cream to brown spots.	Manzeb. Spray at first sign of infection and again 10 days later.	Pick and burn affected foliage.
Powdery mildew.	Appears as a white powdery covering on young leaves, fruits, and vegetables, e.g. tamarillos. Occurs in dry seasons and dry climates.	Bravo. Spray every 14–21 days during summer.	Two teaspoons of baking soda per 2.5 litres of water.
Red thread, fairy rings etc.	Poorly drained soil. Occurs mainly in wet climatic conditions.	Thiram. Spray affected area every 7 days until controlled.	Use fork or aerator to open lawn area.

Black Spot.

Die back.

Hebe after downy mildew attack.

Caterpillar damage.

Problem	Diagnosis	Treatment	Natural Treatment
Black spot.	Causes distorted growth and spotting on apples, pears, roses and ornamentals. In severe cases leaf/fruit drop occurs.	Spray with fungus fighter.	Collect and burn affected material as dormant spores over winter will reinfect spring growth. A dusting of flowers of sulphur will help.
Brown rot on peaches, nectarines, apricots and plums.	All stone fruit can be affected in spring. Flowers/immature fruit often take on a mummified appearance.	Spray with saprol.	Collect and burn affected material.
Pythium. Damping off - on seedlings.	Sudden collapse of young seedlings.	Spray with captan.	Poor light, ventilation and drainage are generally the cause. Rectify the situation and hey presto, success – no problems.
Die-back (shot hole).	Attacks leaves, fruits and twigs. Can cause scabs on fruit.	Copper spray in winter.	Cut out infected material and burn.
Leaf curl. Bladder plum.	Leaves curl as they unfold – severe on stone fruits – causing defoliation and fruit drop. In plums seen as deformed and bladder-like fruit. Affects azaleas also.	Copper spray. Winter, autumn and spring.	Cut out infected leaves and fruit.

Troubleshooting LEAVES

Problem	Symptom	Cause	Treatment
Wilting	General limpness of leaf tissue and/or tip of leaf	Either shortage or too much water, a root problem of pest or disease.	Check drainage. Drench with Shield.
Discolouration.	Black deposit – sooty in appearance. Reddish hues. Loss of colour.	Sooty mould excretion of insects. Irregular watering. Either too wet, too dry, or nutritional.	Spray with all seasons oil of summer strength. Feed with Miracle-Gro.
Mouldy.	Upper surface having greyish deposits. Whitish deposits under surface.	Mildew. Downy mildew.	Spray with Mavrik. Spray with Bravo.
Curled leaves.	Tightly rolled spring tip growth. Curled and discoloured on peaches, nectarines.	Leaf roller caterpillar. Leaf curl.	Spray with orthene. Spray with Super Copper.
Cobwebbing.	Tiny strands of webbing causing wilting and often silvery appearance.	Red Spider mites.	Spray with Miticide.
Spots.	Underside of leaves covered in reddish brown small pustules.	Rust.	Spray with manzeb. Dust with flowers of sulphur.

Troubleshooting LEAVES CONTINUED

Problem	Symptom	Cause	Treatment
Infested with insects.	White, tiny insects – touch the leaves and a cloud of insects will billow out of their hiding places.	Whitefly.	Spray with Mavrik.
	Common on tip growth and buds. Small clusters – green, gray, black & orange in colour.	Aphids.	Spray with Pyrethrum.
	Holes in leaves. Can be elongated, round or with ripped edges.	Caterpillars, beetles, slugs and snails.	Put slug bait around base of plant. Spray with carbaryl.
	Appear on leaves and bark. White and woolly.	Mealy bugs.	Spray with all seasons oil.
	Appear on leaves and stems. Flat brown/black leech-like or star-shaped bug, whitish in colour.	Scale.	Spray with.all seasons oil and malathion.

Troubleshooting FRUIT

Problem	Symptom	Cause	Treatment
Chewed.	Fruit shows irregular eaten damage.	Slugs, wasps and birds.	Slugbait. Cover with bird netting.
Distorted.	Roundish blackish bumps (apples).	Black Spot.	Spray with Bravo.
	Eczema/wart-like lesions (citrus).	Varicosis.	Spray with all seasons oil or copper oxychloride
	Splitting of ripening fruit (tomatoes).	Erratic watering.	Regular deep watering.
	Uneven ripening.	Nutritional - Potash deficiency.	Apply sulphate of potash.
Mouldy.	Brownish blotching which makes fruit unpalatable, e.g. on tomatoes and potatoes.	Blight.	Spray with Super Copper.
	Mould on fruit trees.	Brown rot.	Spray with saprol.
Early fruit drop.	Citrus, stone and pip fruit – early fall.	Frost. Poor drainage, too wet, too dry, climatic.	Cover with Frost cloth.
Insect damage.	Eaten – tree fruits, vegetables, small fruits.	Caterpillars. Codlin Moth. Beetles.	Spray with carbaryl.

Rust.

Aphids.

Whitefly.

Sooty mould on citrus.

Troubleshooting FLOWERS

Problem	Symptom	Cause	Treatment
Dropping or dropping early.	Flowers suddenly dropping.	Short of water, over watering.	Keep damp to the touch.
Discoloured.	Flowers have powdery appearance.	Powdery mildew.	Spray with Bravo.
Distorted.	Misshapen, or fail to open.	Thrips.	Spray with Confidor.
Brown and sludgy at base of bloom.	Collapse at base and fail to open.	Botrytis.	Spray with Bravo.
Shredded.	Masses of holes or pieces ripped.	Caterpillar.	Spray with Mavrik.

Troubleshooting STEMS

Problem	Symptom	Cause	Treatment
Eaten through.	Collapse of young annuals, established and young trees, perennials.	Slugs, snails, rabbits and possum.	Snail bait. Spray with thiram or use a liquid fish fertiliser such as Alaslea.
Sudden death.	Collapse of plant – annuals and vegetables.	Phytophera or Botrytis. Fungal problem. Frost – extreme cold has same effect.	Remove dead material and dust at ground level with flower of sulphur.
Abnormal growth.	Brain-like lesions (spherical blisters) on Wattles and Roses at the base of the stem.	Moth gall or canker.	No cure. Cut out affected material and burn.
Insect damage.	Green, grey, black or orange coloured insects	Aphids.	Spray with Pyrethrum.
	White fluffy-like insect on bark or leaf.	Woolly aphids.	Spray with carbaryl.
	Flat brown/black leech-like or star-shaped bug whitish in colour.	Scale.	Spray with all seasons oil at summer strength.
	Fat worm-like six legged chewer – all shapes and sizes.	Caterpillar.	Spray with carbaryl or Malathion.

Troubleshooting ROOTS & BULBS

Problem	Symptom	Cause	Treatment
Distorted tubers.	Root crops, parsnips, carrots etc being misshapen.	Heavy clay or soil.	Aerate soil by adding coarse sand and compost. Dig in Gypsum to spade depth.
Irregular swellings on roots.	Brassicas and wallflowers – nodular growth inhibits development.	Clubroot.	Drench area with Greenguard and apply lime.
Parts eaten away and poor development.	Basal roots (base) eaten. Organism collapses – blind flowering.	Small soil pests. Millipedes, grass grubs, narcissus fly, leatherjackets.	Apply diazinon granules.

Troubleshooting NUTRITIONAL PROBLEMS

Symptom	Plants Affected	Deficiency	Treatment
Pale foliage or tints of purple/yellow on older leaves is the first symptom.	All leafy vegetables and annuals.	Nitrogen.	Apply Nitrosol as liquid feed. Miracle-Gro and Thrive are others.
Small leaves can show early autumn tints.	Most crops, fruit trees and ornamentals.	Phosphorus.	General garden fertiliser will remedy.
Leaves curl and become scorched.	All leafy vegetables, tomatoes and most fruits.	Potassium.	Apply sulphate of potash or rose fertiliser.
Tips of young leaves curl inward.	Lettuce and celery.	Calcium.	Dolomite or lime application.
Yellowing between leaf veins, pale leaves.	Apples, lettuce, tomatoes, all brassicas.	Magnesium.	Dolomite or, for a quick fix, Magnesium Sulphate.
Bleaching or yellowing veining on young leaves.	Rhododendron, roses, camellias, hydrangeas and small berry fruits.	Iron.	Dissolve breakfast cup of Iron Sulphate in 4.5 litres of water and apply.
Whiptail imperfect growth.	Cauliflowers, bean sprouts, most brassicas.	Molybdenum.	Apply trace elements mix. 750grams covers 45 sq metres.

Viral disease on camellia.

Mildew on rhododendron.

Healthy rhododendron.

Spider mite on viburnum tinus.

Sooty mould – close up.

Annuals, perennials and bulbs

ANNUALS – ideal for the weekend and once-a-month gardener.

Annuals are generally easy care plants that flower and seed all in one season. They are ideal for filling up those vacant garden spaces. The advent of potted colour (i.e. individual plants, already flowering and ready to plant out, giving an instant display) has made it easy for many of us to change or add colour to our gardens.

REMEDIES FOR POOR GROWTH

Most annuals enjoy an open sunny situation. They grow rapidly so soils should be free draining with plenty of compost and fertiliser – blood and bone coupled with a dressing of a general fertiliser at the time of planting or when preparing the soil is essential.

Sweet pea, carnations, sweet william, stock and dianthus all love an alkaline soil, so dolomite has to be incorporated to ensure healthy plants and an abundance of flowers.

Unless you are going for a wildflower look, planting your annuals too close will result in straggly, leggy growth and poor flower production. To avoid this, my rule for annuals which grow no more than 30cm in height is to plant them a hand span apart – double the distance if you are growing taller annuals.

Stunted growth can also be a sign of poor soil, or may indicate the soil is burned out or too compacted. This can be due to the same species being planted in the same place year after year. To solve these problems open up the soil by digging it over and then add one bucket of coarse sand and three buckets of mushroom compost per square metre. If at all possible raise the bed to promote good drainage. For best results rotate annual plantings – e.g. follow pansies with nemesia, then petunias and then back to pansies.

Did you know? A sudden dropping of your impatiens is a sure indication they need watering – a great time to check all your annuals.

Uneven plant growth is often linked to poor nutrition. Ensure you apply a

Annuals, perennials and bulbs

c o n t i n u e d

general fertiliser such as Yates General Garden Fertiliser before planting, spreading the fertiliser evenly to ensure uniform plant growth. A healthy application is generally considered to be a good handful every square metre.

REMEDIES FOR POOR FLOWERING

Often the result of poor soil or it may be that you have placed your plant in the wrong place (a shade loving plant in full sun or vice versa – check labels carefully before planting to see whether they require sun or need shade to flower at their best).

Poor flowering can also be the result of the same species of plant(s) grown year after year in the same area e.g. petunias on top of petunias.

> *Did you know? Asters make great companions to other annuals – keeps them free from insect problems in autumn.*

Pansies are another annual which do not like being planted in the same soil year after year. Often the soil can

become exhausted, as the first season's plantings will take out many of the essential trace elements and nutrients needed for that species. I recommend you rotate your plants every season. If, however, you are like me and are determined to have a pansy or three in your garden all year every year, you need to dig the site over well before each planting, adding organic matter such as sheep pellets. At the same time apply generous amounts of a fertiliser with trace elements like Debco's Rose Fertiliser. Be careful in your choice of fertiliser as not all garden fertilisers contain trace elements.

> **GREAT IDEA:** *Nasturtiums inhibit insects and their young seeds are excellent as poor man's capers. The nasturtium's flowers and young leaves are excellent in salads and sandwiches.*

Poor repeat flowering can result from not removing spent flower heads. Dead-heading can be time consuming if you have lots of flowers, but it is worth the effort.

If you have covered all of the above

Annuals, perennials and bulbs

c o n t i n u e d

then try a teaspoon of dried blood (watered in well) for each plant. This is the quickest means of getting nitrogen to the plant and is a sure-fire way of kick-starting flower production.

> **TOP TIP:** *Watering annuals in containers. Change soil annually and also paint the inside of your pots to slow down evaporation. (I use a product called Terracoat with great success – use bucket-size pots or larger.) Feed your annuals monthly while they are growing with general fertiliser such as Miracle Gro.*

All leaf and few flowers means you have too much nitrogen and may have overdosed on nitrogen-rich fertilisers or blood and bone. To counter this add 50 grams per square metre of super phosphate and stop using anything with nitrogen for a season or two.

REMEDIES FOR PLANTS WILTING, YELLOWING AND DYING

This is usually caused by plants being in an area which is either too shady, too dry or too wet. The first step to take is to aerate your soil. Push a garden fork into the soil but don't turn the soil over. Aim for a depth of 10cms or so. Apply a liquid plant food such as Miracle Gro. If the soil is dry, add some peat as well – a bucketful every square metre. Water the peat well before applying to soil.

If the area is constantly dry then you need regular deep watering – maybe it's time to consider an irrigation system. (Plassay is ideal for this.) If the problem area is damp the best solution is to raise the garden bed and put a drainage system in. If the area is excessively shady and damp you need to open it up to the sunlight - but if this is not possible change your plant selection to those which love the shade and the damp. If the soil is too wet annuals can develop root rot, causing them to collapse completely. Mimulus (monkey flowers), primula and cineraria give a great colour boost to shady, damp areas and are easy to care for as well.

COMMON INSECT PESTS

Aphid, mites, caterpillars, slugs, snails and spittlebug. *(Refer to pages 60–62 for treatment.)*

Annuals, perennials and bulbs

c o n t i n u e d

GREAT IDEA: *Gather the spent seed heads off your annuals, dry them, and store the seeds in a paper bag in a cool dry situation – a most economical way to ensure a bright display for the next season. If you want a wildflower effect then cornflowers, cosmos, marigolds, alyssum and lobelia are all great for scattering in spring.*

Placing your garden beds in an open situation to allow for good ventilation may help reduce the incidence of disease and pests.

COMMON DISEASES

Fusarium or – if soil too wet – root rot, rust or powdery mildew.

Good air movement around each of your plants reduces the likelihood of most common diseases. (*Refer to "Troubleshooting Charts".*)

HANDY HINT: *The delightful French marigold repels aphids and protects potatoes and tomatoes from disease.*

Annuals, perennials and bulbs

c o n t i n u e d

PERENNIALS – ideal for all gardeners. Perennials are permanent and, by carefully choosing types and forms, a colourful display can be achieved for most of the year.

REMEDIES FOR POOR GROWTH

Perennials are gross feeders requiring plenty of organic matter to be worked into the garden beds before planting. They prefer a free draining situation, so raise your garden beds. Adding a little drainage to the beds is a great idea as well.

Many perennials need staking, e.g. delphiniums, hollyhocks, asters and phlox. Some, like hollyhock and sweet peas, enjoy growing near a brick wall. The heat given off by the wall will encourage these perennials to give a wondrous display.

Straggly growth is caused by over-crowding or by a shady situation. Keep space around your plants (two hand spans apart), don't overplant.

Overcrowding will ultimately cause your plant to collapse. If this happens, lift the crown of your plant, keeping only the strongest outer shoots for replanting. Important with chrysanthemums, iris and helianthus.

> **HANDY HINT:** *After that weekend party you should apply the left over dregs of beer or wine to your plants – they love the nutrients – but dilute 50:50 with water.*

Most perennials are sun lovers. If they are planted in too much shade they will not thrive and will become leggy, as they tend to stretch towards the sun.

Check plant labels for the correct placement of your perennials.

Shade-loving perennials are poor performers in the heat and will scorch in the sun. Plant in dappled shade.

All clumping perennials need to be divided every two to three years, with the exception of peonies. If not divided the plants will become stunted and lose vigour, resulting in poor flowering.

Stunted growth is a sign of not enough nutrients. Perennials are gross feeders – they need mulching and dividing during winter to prepare for

Annuals, perennials and bulbs

c o n t i n u e d

their spring growth. Apply general garden fertiliser (50gms per sq m) in spring, midsummer and, for good measure, half this amount in early autumn.

REMEDIES FOR POOR FLOWERING

Overcrowding is the most common cause of poor flowering, as the roots of each plant struggle to gain the food they need. Lift and divide your plants in late autumn before they completely die down, and replant using only the strongest divisions. Reject old woody central crowns. All perennials flower on new season growth.

> **TOP TIP:** *Pyrethrum, daisies and wormwood repel insects. Plant around your barbecue area or outside your kitchen. Keeps those mosquitoes and flies away.*

Perennials should have spent flower stems removed once each flower has finished. If this step is not followed the plants put their energy into making seeds and will not flush with flowers again. A good example of this is delphiniums.

All leaf and few flowers usually means too much nitrogen. Cut back on your application of blood and bone and nitrogen-based fertilisers.

Liquid feeding with a balanced flower-promoting fertiliser such as Debco Flower Booster each month, from September through to March, ensures healthy, vigorous plants.

> **HANDY HINT:** *Soak anenome and ranunculus corms for four hours before planting into potting mix for better germination - but they don't like each other so don't plant them together.*

REMEDIES FOR WILTING, YELLOWING AND DYING

Usually this problem is caused by a root disorder. It is best to dig up the plant and discard anything that looks diseased and tatty. Lightly dust the root area with flowers of sulphur to reduce infection. Don't replant the same variety in the same spot. If the problem continues, replace the plant. Open up the soil to let

Annuals, perennials and bulbs

c o n t i n u e d

the air into the affected area and leave undisturbed for a week or two.

COMMON INSECT PESTS

Aphid, whitefly, mites and thrips. (*Refer to pages 60–62 for treatment.*)

Watch for slug and snail damage - snail bait is essential.

COMMON DISEASES

Sooty mould, mildew and rust. (*Refer to "Troubleshooting Charts".*)

> **HANDY HINT:** *To prevent your plants drying out and to save on watering, use a mulch through the hot summer months while growth is in progress. A good tip is to always water the bed well before laying down your mulch.*

BULBS – great for all gardening styles!

REMEDIES FOR POOR GROWTH

An open, free draining site is essential for most bulbs. They will not thrive with wet feet. Most bulbs should be planted at twice their depth – the exception are nerines and amaryllis which like the neck of their bulbs above the ground.

> **HANDY HINT:** *Plant bulbs of the same colour – they will all flower together, giving a much better display.*

Where soil is heavy add a handful of coarse sand under each bulb before planting to help with drainage. Bulbs enjoy a soil rich in potash – this can be achieved by using packs of specially formulated Bulb Food fertilisers, sulphate of potash or rose fertiliser at the rate of 150gms per square metre. Apply fertilisers when planting your bulbs, again when the flower spike appears and again immediately after flowering – but at the lesser rate of 50gms per square metre.

Taller growing bulbs such as gladioli and iris should be planted in groups of 5, 7 or 9 and at a distance twice the width of the bulb (this closeness helps to support the flowers on windy days). Another means of support is to position garden stakes at planting time. For

Annuals, perennials and bulbs

c o n t i n u e d

supporting smaller growers like freesias a hoop stake is excellent.

REMEDIES FOR POOR FLOWERING

Lack of flowers from your bulbs is usually because no fertiliser has been added to the soil after the previous season's flowering. Fertilising when the flower has just finished is crucial, as at that stage all bulbs are laying the foundation for the next season's flower. This is particularly important if your bulbs are clumping.

Other possible reasons for the lack of flowers from healthy bulbs are overcrowding, too much shade or late planting. Overcrowding can be easily identified by spindly growth with lime-green foliage or maybe yellow leaves at the base of the plant. If your bulbs are overcrowded or in too much shade, lift them and relocate to a sunny location.

> **GREAT IDEA:** *When rinsing those supermarket meat trays, retain the liquid and use as a natural food — bulbs love it.*

Undersized bulbs are juveniles and will not flower for a year or two – such bulbs are often heavily discounted at the garden supply shops, so buy your bulbs early in the season to avoid being left with the small ones.

All leaf is a sign of too much nitrogen – reduce your use of nitrogen-rich fertiliser. It can also be a sign of stress – have you planted your bulbs in too shady a spot?

Deformed flowers can be caused by the climate – for example, if it has been too cold as the bud is developing, the bud can rot or fail to open. More often though, deformed flowers and greying leaves occur in warmer climates and are caused by thrips sucking the juices out of the plant just as bud production is under way. This commonly occurs with gladioli, iris, spraxias, freesias and ixias.

REMEDIES FOR PLANTS WILTING, YELLOWING AND DYING

Yellowing foliage is a sign of either a nutritional problem or that the bulbs have wet feet. To remedy the first problem apply general fertiliser in late

Diseased and damaged bulbs.

Tulips in full bloom.

Hosta plantaginea – control slugs and snails and your hosta leaves will remain in one piece.

Polyanthus – healthy example.

Carnation – fungal disease.

Annuals, perennials and bulbs

c o n t i n u e d

summer/autumn and use a good bulb food again in spring. Wet feet? Well there is only one thing to do – find a drier area to plant your bulbs.

TOP TIP: *Charcoal added to undrained containers stops root rot.*

Stunted growth with yellow tips that then die back is usually caused by root rot or insects.

If root rot is the problem the best solution is to dump the bulbs and fix the site. Coarse sand is an ideal medium to use for good drainage.

COMMON INSECT PESTS

Aphid, bulb fly infestation, thrips, slugs and snails. *(Refer to pages 60–62 for treatment.)*

COMMON DISEASES

Rust, pythium and mildew. *(Refer to "Troubleshooting Charts".)*

It is important to note that bulbs need a cold snap to start growth and to help them develop. In warm areas I recommend buying tulip and hyacinth bulbs when they are fresh and storing in a brown paper bag for 4–6 weeks (in the fridge – not freezer) and then planting out.

If this is not practical, plant the bulbs then throw ice over the ground every three weeks until they poke their heads through the ground. (This is particularly important with tulips.)

When choosing bulbs buy early in the season. It is so important to select firm, plump, sound bulbs. For planting in a paddock or a lawn, throw them in the air and plant them where they fall. This gives a more natural effect than grid planting. (Using a bulb planter tool makes the job easier.)

Raised beds give best results – rockeries and containers are great for smaller types such as crocus. They reduce the risk of wet feet.

GREAT IDEA: *Use whole cloves at the base of your bulb pots – keep those ants at bay.*

House plants, palms and succulents

Many think of house plants as disposable items. However, this doesn't necessarily have to be the case. Poor watering is the major cause of the demise of our plants – either too much, too little or too late. How often have you forgotten that plant until it is no more than a mass of dead leaves?

REMEDIES FOR POOR GROWTH

This usually happens when you put your precious plant in a position that is either too dark or where it receives far too much sun. It could also be that the plant is too wet or too dry.

A plant situated in the wrong place is fairly easy to detect. The leaves lose their lustre, start to wilt, become elongated and sometimes burn at the edges or tips.

Straggly growth is often a sign of the plant having to stretch towards the sunlight. Fortunately this is easily remedied by rotating your plant or changing its position to somewhere with better light.

Poor growth can also be the result of a lack of food. To keep your house plants in peak condition a monthly feeding programme should be adhered to – even over the winter months. Miracle Gro fertiliser is my choice.

> **GREAT IDEA:** *A Peace Lily growing amongst your indoor plants is the ideal indicator plant. They droop noticeably when they need water – this is the ideal time to water all your house plants.*

With modern heating systems, homes often have too much dry air for plants to flourish. Keep the air humid by placing a tray with pebbles under potted plants. Fill with warm water and check every second day. Refill when necessary.

> **HANDY HINT:** *African violets love heat, steam and good light. Water with tepid water for increased flowering – but never water the leaves.*

Too much water can also be a problem. A frequent light watering is better, cutting down over the winter months. For the majority of plants you can get away with placing them in a sink full of water and waiting for the air

House plants, palms and succulents

c o n t i n u e d

bubbles to dissipate. Done once a week in summer, this is the perfect way to keep your plants healthy.

Remove all dead growth from the plant and surrounding soil as soon as you spot it. Leaving dead leaves around attracts bugs and diseases.

REMEDIES FOR POOR FLOWERING

The usual causes are not enough light or lack of nutrients, depending on the type of plant. Poor flowering is often aligned with straggly growth.

Too much nitrogen can also be the culprit. To facilitate flowering use a liquid feed with a high potash concentration, as that promotes bud development and flowers.

> **Did you know?** To clean the leaves of glossy foliaged house plants, use a 50:50 mix of water and milk and wipe the leaves gently. Also elkhorn and staghorn ferns love chopped banana skins dropped into the back of their crowns. It brings colour back into their leaves.

Remove spent flowers as soon as they are finished, as this prevents decay and encourages new bud growth. Cyclamen, in particular, benefit from this treatment.

REMEDIES FOR WILTING, YELLOWING AND DYING

Yellowing of foliage is mainly due to poor light, ventilation, nutrition or, heaven forbid, all three. If you are feeding your plant well but it is still yellowing, place the plant in a more open, ventilated position, and if the soil is wet to touch then reduce watering.

Wilting on new growth is a sign that the plant is too dry. Increase your watering and feed with liquid plant food.

COMMON INSECT PESTS

Scale, mealy bug, thrips, mites and aphids. *(Refer to pages 60–62 for treatment.)*

COMMON DISEASES

Mildew, botrytis. *(Refer to "Troubleshooting Charts".)*

House plants, palms and succulents

c o n t i n u e d

HANDY HINT: *Flowering indoor plants such as cyclamen, polyanthus, kalanchoe, chrysanthemums and poinsettia – always grow two and rotate inside-outside every three to four days (weather permitting). Cool, well lit situations are best – don't put into full sun or burning of flowers and foliage can occur.*

FERNS & PALMS

REMEDIES FOR POOR GROWTH

Usually due to moisture deprivation – all ferns and palms need their roots to be cool and moist. A sudden change in these conditions will result in yellowing and, in extreme cases, death.

REMEDIES FOR PLANTS WILTING, YELLOWING AND DYING

Drying out or too much warmth on the roots will result in yellowing off, leaves dropping and, in some cases, death. So keep the humidity up – don't let your plants dry out for too long. Spray with an atomizer sprayer three or four times a week.

Allowing the roots of your palms to become cold will cause yellowing and wilting as well. Add some stones to the saucer your plant is standing on to keep the roots well away from water. Shift plants to another position.

GREAT IDEA: *After you have boiled eggs – keep that water until it is cold and water your ferns with it. Helps with colour and vigour - maidenhair ferns love it. The salt or vinegar in the water is also great as a tonic.*

COMMON INSECT PESTS

Scale, mealy bugs. *(Refer to pages 60–62 for treatment.)*

COMMON DISEASES

Botrytis. *(Refer to "Troubleshooting Charts".)*

TOP TIP: *Mealy bug a problem? Apply methylated spirits to the affected area with a child's paintbrush.*

Root-bound plant.

Healthy fern.

Healthy succulents make striking plants.

Aloe ferox.

Sedum pachyohyllum.

House plants, palms and succulents

c o n t i n u e d

SUCCULENTS

This forgiving, enchanting group of plants love the sun. Many won't tolerate frost so positioning is important – whether grown in containers, which they love, or as garden subjects.

REMEDIES FOR POOR GROWTH

A free draining soil type is essential. Too wet and your succulents will collapse – too dry and they will be distorted. Uneven light can also cause distortion.

Regular feeding and watering is essential. Hand watering is best every 10–14 days during winter.

Succulents will grow in minimal soil. Anything that can contain potting mix can grow succulents – old shoes, pots and pans, china, glassware, the choice is yours.

Place in a position protected from frost – the hotter the better, they hate shade!

REMEDIES FOR POOR FLOWERING

The flower stems in some varieties should be removed the moment you notice them. If left to flower they will retard the look and development of your specimen - especially important when growing the large echeveria.

Sedum, on the other hand, is more tolerant and will give a spectacular display when in flower.

REMEDIES FOR PLANTS WILTING, YELLOWING AND DYING

Collapse – your succulents are either too dry or too wet. Dry out the plants. They don't like to have wet feet. Put extra drainage in the container or, if planted outside, make sure they are in a northern or easterly aspect. Obviously if they are too dry then water them carefully.

COMMON INSECT PESTS

Mealy bug and red spider are the two most common pests that will affect your succulents. Be warned though, slugs and snails will find the fleshy leaves appetizing. *(Refer to pages 60–62 for treatment.)*

COMMON DISEASES

Mildew. *(Refer to "Troubleshooting Charts".)*

Climbers, roses and orchids

CLIMBERS

Climbers – from the frost tender to hardy, deciduous to evergreen, there is a climber for every situation and they are well worth growing. Used in trees, with roses, over a shed, a fence or growing on the house, the effects of climbers can be spectacular.

REMEDIES FOR POOR GROWTH

The secret to climbers is they don't like to be cultivated around the root area – this is the main reason for poor development.

All climbers need some sort of support – this can be man-made or natural.

Clematis enjoys a cool root run if planted out in the open. Water well and place a few stones or bricks around the base of the plant to keep the roots cool.

> **GREAT IDEA:** *An inexpensive way to attach a climber to a fence is to use large cup hooks and string fishing nylon through. When you want to paint the fence it will be easy to release and put back when the paint is dry.*

Suckering or rampant growth from the base of some climbers is natural. In their wild state this ensures the plant's survival. To remedy suckering pull off the growth rather than cut back. By pulling the suckers off there is little chance of regrowth – cutting back will only stimulate the dormant buds and encourage more growth.

For most flowering climbers prune after flowering. However take care as woody climbers such as wisteria flower on the previous season's growth.

Winter flowering climbers are best fertilised with a general garden fertiliser such as Nitrophoska Blue in early autumn and mid summer. Fertilise in early autumn and late winter for spring and summer flowering climbers.

REMEDIES FOR POOR FLOWERING

Clematis and wisteria like a lime soil, and will benefit from a light handful of dolomite applied in late winter – this heightens the colour and promotes flower bud development. However most other climbers like an acidic soil, so

Climbers, roses and orchids

c o n t i n u e d

fertilise with a spring dressing of Yates Acid Fertiliser.

The majority of climbers flower on the current season's growth, and all should be pruned when flowering ceases, or in early spring for those which are frost prone such as bougainvillaea or akebia.

Tropical climbers like a free draining soil. Others e.g. clematis, enjoy a cool root run, but not wet feet. If the ground moisture is poor the edges of the foliage will burn and flower buds may drop or be disfigured.

Poor flowering is often due to pruning at the wrong time and · inadvertently cutting off the potential flowering growth. The other reason is too much nitrogenous fertiliser, e.g. blood and bone or Nitrosol (a liquid blood and bone). If none of these apply and you still have no flowers my bet is the plant is trying to grow in too much shade – so shift it.

All foliage and no flowers – very depressing – is probably due to too much fertiliser, which stimulates leaf growth at the expense of flowering.

Most climbers will have poor flowering if over-fed. (Keep them keen by feeding mean.)

> **GREAT IDEA:** *Don't waste grapefruit skins – invert them and place around the bottom of climbers – they make excellent slug traps.*

REMEDIES FOR PLANTS WILTING, YELLOWING AND DYING

If the tips of your climbers start to wilt then the root area is either too wet or too dry. This is a common problem that if not remedied will result in further wilting, yellowing and eventual collapse.

Many climbers can collapse overnight if the conditions become too adverse so check the growing instructions and site before planting. Hardier specimens such as wisteria, jasmine and the potato vine can withstand most conditions. Be warned – frost is a major problem with tropical climbers like bougainvillaea.

If none of the above conditions are evident it may be that a fungal disease or borer is attacking your climber.

If it is too dry, water well and then

Climbers, roses and orchids

c o n t i n u e d

place a few stones or bricks around the base of your plant to act as a barrier to evaporation and sun. If your climber is too wet I suggest you shift it on a cool, cloudy day. Cut back by two thirds a week or so (if possible) before moving.

> **TOP TIP:** *Stop your wisteria buds from becoming bird nest liners by draping cotton threads through the climber.*

COMMON INSECT PESTS

Scale, mealy bug, borer, slugs and snails. *(Refer to pages 60–62 for treatment.)*

COMMON DISEASES

Blackspot, mildew. *(Refer to "Troubleshooting Charts".)*

> **HANDY HINT:** *Birds continue to be a problem on your wisteria? the fluffy buds get pecked and used for nest liners. Dust with cayenne pepper or spray with thiram to give some protection - if this fails then take a country music CD and play it loudly, this will surely scare most things away.*

ROSES

Considered to be the queen of flowers, from tiny miniatures to rambling giants – the choice today is mind-boggling.

Today's scientific breeding programmes mean more resistance to disease, freer-flowering roses, and varieties which will thrive in normally difficult situations, e.g. semi-shade.

REMEDIES FOR POOR GROWTH

Burning on the leaves is often water related. Water at the root area, not over the foliage. The best time for watering is when the sun is off your plants.

Straggly growth, depending on type, can be a result of poor pruning and/or the rose bush being planted too high. If it is straggly growth make sure the crown of the rose is at soil level and ensure pruning is carried out correctly and at the right time.

Make sure there is good air movement and watering is at regular intervals.

Roses – healthy flowers and leaves.

Powdery mildew.

Cymbidium orchids.

Clematis (Mrs James Mason).

Climbers, roses and orchids

c o n t i n u e d

REMEDIES FOR POOR FLOWERING

Dead-heading all spent blooms is a must to increase flowering.

To increase depth of colour in your roses, extra potash can be applied. Sheep pellets and liquid fish fertiliser are also beneficial. The latter keeps the possums away as well.

TOP TIP: *Coffee grounds are an excellent way of increasing soil texture around your roses – a great way to recycle and suppress weeds to boot!*

Poor flowering is often due to poor position (too shady), nutritional deficiencies or overcrowding the area with other plants. Check position and space and feed regularly with a balanced rose food.

Roses love the sun – put them in a site that ensures them heaps.

For pruning without worry grow the "Fairy" or flower carpet forms – all you need is hedge shears. No pain and all gain!

TOP TIP: *Garlic planted by each rose bush dispels aphids.*

All leaf and no flowers is due to the soil being too high in nitrates.

Distorted flowering can also be the result of insect damage or a fungal infection.

REMEDIES FOR PLANTS WILTING, YELLOWING AND DYING

Wilting is more likely to be a root-induced fungal problem rather than a watering problem, as roses can tolerate a good degree of dryness.

Yellowing of leaves is often a magnesium deficiency.

Pinking around the edge of the leaves indicates a phosphorus deficiency.

Planting too close or poor pruning results in the bottom leaves going yellow and dropping off.

Climbers, roses and orchids

c o n t i n u e d

An unhealthy specimen is hardly worth the effort – pull it out and burn.

COMMON INSECT PESTS

Aphids, scale, mealy bug, thrips and mites. (*Refer to pages 60–62 for treatment.*)

COMMON DISEASES

Black spot, rust, mildew. (*Refer to "Troubleshooting Charts".*)

ORCHIDS (Cymbidium)

These tropical jewels suffer from the popular misconception that they are difficult to grow and need extra special care. Well it's about time we dispelled some of these myths.

In their natural habitat orchids are epiphytes, anchoring themselves on branches and growing in the forest canopy, where they draw their nourishment from rain and decomposing plant litter.

REMEDIES FOR POOR GROWTH

This can be caused by your orchids being too wet, too dry or a lack of food – but generally it's just total neglect.

Orchids thrive in a coarse free-draining soil type – commercial mixes are available and contain bark/pumice and slow release fertiliser.

They can be propagated by division or back bulbs. The latter are spent flowering corms (which are storage organs). Once removed they are placed in coarse open mix and, providing they are firm, will send a shoot from the side in spring and flower in the third year.

Over-crowded, potted specimens should be divided every two years after flowering has ceased. Divide and replant after flowering (around October/November).

Although frost tender, they can also be grown outside successfully – preferably in a semi-shade position.

REMEDIES FOR POOR FLOWERING

This can be due to the orchid flowers being left on the plant to seed. If this has been the case flowering will be reduced for the following season. Cut spent flower heads from your orchid as soon as practical.

Climbers, roses and orchids

c o n t i n u e d

Too often orchids are neglected; they've been brought inside to flower and once they have finished flowering they are put outside again and forgotten. To promote flowering they need a programme of feeding. This is very easy – use Biotissue Orchid Food monthly.

At the pre-flowering stage spray with copper oxychloride once a month to combat any fungal problem such as black spot. Make sure there is good ventilation for your plant and don't spray once the flower spike has broken through its protective sheath – you'll damage the buds.

All leaf and no flower usually means too much nitrogen so cut back on fertilising your plants with Nitrosol or blood and bone.

REMEDIES FOR PLANTS WILTING, YELLOWING AND DYING

Yellowing of leaves is a regular feature of orchids grown outdoors. A monthly application of a balanced fertiliser and an application of blood and bone remedies this.

If you are feeding them well and the leaves are still yellow, move your plant to a semi-shaded situation that is well ventilated. Outside, under the canopy of an existing tree, is always a good spot.

Burned tips on the leaves is a sign of irregular watering – aim to water every week during summer and every two weeks in winter. You can liquid feed at the same time.

COMMON INSECT PESTS

Scale, aphids, mealy bug, mite and thrips. (*Refer to pages 60–62 for treatment.*)

COMMON DISEASES

Black spot, bacterial root rot. (*Refer to "Troubleshooting Charts".*)

I love orchids and most years I have many growing inside my home. If you're growing them outside beware. Slugs and snails love the new flower spikes – so be vigilant with your snail and slug baiting.

Trees, shrubs and NZ natives

TREES

The backbone of all gardens.

REMEDIES FOR POOR GROWTH

Can be due to being planted too close - for every 10 metres in eventual height leave a gap of 5 metres. Poor growth is often due to the tree not being planted deep enough, firmed in properly or staked – e.g. the tree will move in the wind and new root growth will be damaged, resulting in stunted growth or total collapse.

Planting your tree in too dry or too wet situations will also result in poor growth. These conditions can put the tree under stress, forcing it to put all its efforts into staying alive instead of growing. If your garden is prone to water-logging then raise the level the tree is being planted at.

REMEDIES FOR POOR FLOWERING

Generally a nutritional problem - the available potassium is restricted or there is too much nitrogen. Don't be heavy handed with blood and bone. I find using Magamp or Osmocote plugs at planting is best.

Sometimes poor flowering can be brought about by abrupt climatic changes – warm weather in winter followed by a cold snap. The plant loses its sense of seasons and may sit and do nothing or flower erratically.

REMEDIES FOR PLANTS WILTING, YELLOWING AND DYING

Too dry or too wet are the most common reasons for trees to wilt and die. Wrong soil type is another – if the plant is lime-loving and is planted in an acid soil it will initially grow but once the young feeder roots reach the new soil the tree will begin to wilt, go yellow and collapse.

Fungal or insect damage also causes wilting, yellowing and, in severe cases, death.

Mulching too close to the trunk can cause the tree to sweat, giving the same effect as if you had ring-barked the tree - eventually it will die. Leave at least a

Blistering of leaves on a pittosporum, caused by psyllids.

Pohutukawa in good health.

Leaf hopper.

Mealy bug.

Results of borer mite.

Trees, shrubs and NZ natives

c o n t i n u e d

good hand span between the base of the tree and your mulch, particularly if grass clippings are used. In exposed sites protect your new trees with a windbreak.

Once your trees are established – leave well alone. If light pruning for shape is required, whenever you have the secateurs in your hand is the best time.

COMMON INSECT PESTS

Aphid, slug, pearslug, snail. (*Refer to pages 60–62 for treatment.*)

COMMON DISEASES

Mildew, botrytis, blackspot. (*Refer to "Troubleshooting Charts".*)

SHRUBS

REMEDIES FOR POOR GROWTH

Planting too close is a common reason for poor growth. Shrubs need space to do well – plant at least 1.5 metres apart from each other.

Cultivation around the roots is a no-no as you will rip the plant's feeding roots. Mulching is essential to help the roots take up water and food.

The wrong plant in the wrong site is another major reason for poor growth, as is fertilising for some shrubs – i.e. most Australian and South African natives. They can tolerate Osmocote but collapse quickly when base fertilisers are used. Grevilleas, banksias, leucodendrons and proteas fall into this category.

> **GREAT IDEA:** *A few stems of willow in a bucket of water makes an economical rooting hormone to use on hardwood cuttings.*

REMEDIES FOR POOR FLOWERING

Often an indication the plant has suffered a climatic shock – i.e. too dry and then too wet over a short space of time – due perhaps to weather or erratic watering. Too much or too little water will cause buds to drop rather than develop.

A lush plant with few or no flowers is more often the result of too much nitrogen. Another reason is the shrub

Trees, shrubs and NZ natives

c o n t i n u e d

may be starved of essential elements.

Bud blast is a disease which is the result of wet humid weather. (Flowers fail to open or are distorted and collapse.) This affects early spring to summer flowering shrubs – spray with Bravo to protect the plant from further attacks.

An attack of insects such as aphids that chew or suck the buds will also result in poor flowering – ensure you take measures to prevent this. Shield is a good general fungicide and insecticide which controls most everyday scourges.

REMEDIES FOR PLANTS WILTING, YELLOWING AND DYING

Most shrubs will tolerate the dry (not too dry however) but they will turn their toes up if they get too wet.

Sometimes though, this can be a nutritional problem particularly evident in camellias, daphne and gardenias where leaves yellow on older growth. This is a sign of either iron or magnesium deficiency. Apply a dressing of a level tablespoon of trace element and mix around the drip line of the shrub, watering in well.

Yellowing on younger growth is indicative of an iron deficiency and can be quickly remedied by using Sequestrine. The cause of wilting and yellowing all over the shrub is the dreaded borer.

> **GREAT IDEA:** *Cold tea is excellent for keeping foliage of gardenias and camellias green – the tannin helps. Epsom salts is another economical way to fix yellow leaves on camellias and daphne.*

COMMON INSECT PESTS

Aphids, scale, whitefly, slugs, snails, thrips, borer – in essence a shrub is a veritable salad bar for most insects, so put in place a regular spray programme to protect your plants. (*Refer to pages 60–62 for treatment.*)

COMMON DISEASES

Botrytis, blackspot, mildew are the three most common diseases, followed by rust. (*Refer to "Troubleshooting Charts".*)

Trees, shrubs and NZ natives

c o n t i n u e d

HANDY HINT: *To keep hydrangeas blue, apply aluminium sulphate after mid-spring pruning. For pink; a good handful of lime or dolomite will do the trick.*

NEW ZEALAND NATIVES

REMEDIES FOR POOR GROWTH

Natives adapt to most situations, however some are intolerant of wet feet. Hebes don't like to dry out. A cool root run is preferable – they love mulching.

Cultivation around the roots is another no no, as you will rip the feeding roots. Many natives make good hedges – hebe buxifolia and Jack Hobb's Wiri series are superb as low hedges.

REMEDIES FOR POOR FLOWERING

Too much cultivation is the scourge of natives. If the native plant has suffered a climatic shock – i.e. too dry and then too wet over a very short space of time – it is likely flowers will fail to develop also.

A lush plant with few or no flowers is more often the result of over feeding.

Wilting, yellowing and flowers that fall off can be caused by that beast the native borer – this pest is quite vigorous in its attack and, while often not killing the plant, its flowering is reduced. This problem is particularly prevalent on kowhai, puriri and kaka beak.

REMEDIES FOR PLANTS WILTING, YELLOWING AND DYING

Most problems with natives are nutritional. Apply a sweeping handful of Nitrophosphate Blue every few square metres in spring and autumn.

A dressing of blood and bone will also help stimulate root growth – when planting your natives a handful mixed into the soil in the hole is ideal. If you forget then top feed and water well.

COMMON INSECT PESTS

Caterpillars, borer beetle, scale. *(Refer to pages 60–62 for treatment.)*

COMMON DISEASES

Sooty mould, black spot. *(Refer to "Troubleshooting Charts".)*

Common Insect Pests

Problem	Symptom	Treatment	Natural Treatment
Aphids & Woolly Aphid	Small oval shaped insects usually in clusters on tip growth. Cause distortion and stunted growth and loss of vigour to plants. Attacks fruits, vegetables, ornamentals – even weeds.	- Mavrik (a bee friendly chemical spray).	- Pyrethrum or garlic spray - Wash over with soapy washing water (cold of course). - Squash by hand. - Lady birds - they eat 400 a week.
Borer/Lemon tree	Borer larva tunnels and destroys stem tissue, causing stems and limbs to weaken and die. Attacks citrus, fruit trees, small fruits and a raft of ornamentals. Distinguished by sawdust-like deposits on stems and bark.	- Conqueror Oil (all seasons) spray. - Inject with Kiwicare borer injector fluid.	-Conqueror Oil. - Kerosene poured into entrance holes. Seal with petroleum jelly.
White Butterfly	Attacks cabbage, cauliflower, broccoli, swedes, brussel sprouts. Reduces leaves to skeletons. Caterpillars are dull green in colour and voracious eaters.	- carbaryl. - Pyrethrum. - Derris Dust.	- Squash by hand. - Make up spray by boiling lettuce leaves – cool and apply at rate of 1 to 3.
Carrot Rust Fly	Young seedlings of carrots, parsnips, celery and parsley are stripped bare and it attacks from seedling to maturity.	- Diazinon.	- Jeyes Fluid. - Wind break. - Soapy water wash.
Codlin Moth	Adults fly from October through November. They lay eggs from which caterpillars emerge and attack pip fruit (pears, apples, quince) and related ornamentals.	- Critical to spray October, December and January. - Malathion Spray. - Diazinon granules.	- Wrap corrugated cardboard around trunk impregnated with Petroleum Jelly or insecticide. - Plant tansy, woodruff at base.

Common Insect Pests

Problem	Symptom	Treatment	Natural Treatment
Grass Grub	This root-eating larva of beetles is evident from February to May causing extensive turf damage.	- Diazinon granules.	- Corrugated cardboard impregnated with Petroleum Jelly then attached to trunk of fruit trees.
Green Vegetable Bug	A severe pest of vegetable and garden plants. Loves beans. Distinctive bright green in colour.	- Mavrik insecticide. - Malathion insecticide. - carbaryl insecticide.	- Squash by hand. - Pyrethrum/garlic spray.
Leaf Hopper	White flecking on foliage – often present on the underside of leaves. Hop amongst foliage when disturbed.	- Pyrethrum.	- Garlic Spray (see page 63). - Cold, soapy washing water applied daily until infestation controlled.
Leaf Roller Caterpillar	A surface chewing caterpillar found on fruit trees and ornamental plants. Causes major damage to late fruiting crops resulting in secondary fruit rot.	- carbaryl.	- Squash by hand. - Garlic and Pyrethrum spray.
Mealy Bug	White fluffy insect which causes debilitation and stunted growth. Affects house plants, ornamentals, fruit trees, cacti, palms.	- Confidor (spray or drench). - Maldison and oil.	- Methylated Spirits on paint brush.
Passion Vine Hopper	Yellow to pale green in colour with bell shaped wings - causes severe foliage damage.	- Mavrik (bee friendly insecticide).	- Pyrethrum and garlic spray.
Pear Slug	Small black slimy slug which strips the green off leaves - attacks a wide range of ornamentals and cherry, plum and pear trees.	- Malathion. - carbaryl.	- Pyrethrum and garlic spray.

Common Insect Pests

Problem	Symptom	Treatment	Natural Treatment
Psyllid	Blistering of leaves – attacks pittosporum.	- Orthene. - Pyrethrum.	- Cut and remove if infestation heavy.
Scale Insects (Sooty Mould)	Excretion of scale insects - often on ornamentals and native manuka. Looks like blackish soot.	- Combination of all seasons oil and malathion. Gives good chemical control.	- Wipe off foliage with rag dipped in milk or all seasons oil wash.
Slugs and Snails	Member of octopus and oyster family - love the damp. They cause severe damage to newly planted flower plants, vegetables and seedlings along with a broad number of ornamentals and succulents.	- Mesurol/Baysol.	- Egg shells, crushed and placed around young seedlings. - Flat beer in saucers. - Pick them up at night with a torch and put them in a bucket of hot water, or crush them.
Spider Mite	Dust mites are red in winter. Cause severe stunting and discolouration. Affect herbaceous and woody plants and vegetables.	- Mite Killer.	- Keep plant foliage atomized with water.
Thrips	Pin-size black insects found feeding on the sap on the underside of leaves - resulting in characteristic silvering of foliage. Attacks a wide range of ornamentals.	- Confidor is best, or Spraying oil and malathion.	- Remove affected material.
White Fly	Miniature white sap – sucking moth-like insects which attack almost any plant growth including vegetables, fruits, ornamentals and weeds.	- Confidor. - Target.	- Kodak yellow paper hung with a coating of Petroleum Jelly.

Simple home-made sprays

GARLIC, CHILLI AND ONION SPRAY:

3 chopped onions
10 chopped garlic cloves
5 chopped chillies
1 litre of water
1 teaspoon of dish detergent

METHOD: Boil garlic, chilli and onions in the water for 10 minutes. Leave to stand overnight. Mix in the dish detergent (this helps the liquid to cling to the foliage). Store and use when needed. Make up the spray at a ratio of 1 cup of the solution to 10 litres of water.
Perfect for: Aphids, white butterfly, leaf curl and brown rot.

RHUBARB LEAF SPRAY:

1.5kg rhubarb leaves
5 litres water
15gms good quality soap flakes

METHOD: Boil the chopped rhubarb leaves for half an hour in 3.5 litres of the water, then strain. Dissolve the soap flakes in the remaining water and, when the rhubarb mixture is cold, add the two mixtures together. Perfect for aphids and mildew.

GARLIC SPRAY:

50gms chopped garlic
600mls water
1 teaspoon liquid soap
2 teaspoons kerosene

METHOD: Soak the chopped garlic in the kerosene for 24 hours. (Leave out in the shed.) Dissolve the liquid soap in the water and add to the mixture. Stir well and strain through a stocking into a non-metallic container, and store. To use, dilute one part of the mixture to 20 parts of water.
Perfect for: Aphids, white butterfly, bean fly, leaf curl and brown rot.

HORSE RADISH SPRAY:

Handful of horse radish leaves
Boiling water

METHOD: Pour enough boiling water over the leaves to cover and allow the mixture to infuse for half an hour. Use the mixture immediately at the ratio of four parts water to one part mixture. Spray at the first sign of disease.
Note: Always use the young leaves.
Perfect for brown rot.

Basic monthly spray programme

Check regularly (especially the underside of leaves) for insect or fungal damage, and spray accordingly. If in doubt, take a sample into your local garden centre for remedial advice.

MONTH: | **RIGHT TIME TO SPRAY WITH...**

JANUARY Pip fruit: Manzeb with carbaryl (until harvest).
Stone fruit: Bravo with carbaryl (until harvest).
Roses: Super Shield or Shield.
Tomatoes: Bravo or Tomato Spray (until harvest).

FEBRUARY Citrus: Champion Copper with orthene and Conqueror Oil.
Pip fruit: Manzeb with carbaryl (until harvest).
Stone fruit Bravo with carbaryl (until harvest).
Roses: Super Shield or Shield.

MARCH Take a break and put your feet up.

APRIL Citrus: Champion copper with orthene.
Stone fruit: Champion Copper.

MAY Citrus: Champion Copper with orthene.
Pip fruit: Champion Copper with Conqueror Oil (can be sprayed anytime during the winter months).
Stone fruit: Champion Copper.
Rose: Champion Copper with Conqueror Oil.

JUNE Citrus: Champion Copper with orthene.
Stone fruit: Champion Copper.

JULY Stone fruit: Champion Copper.
Roses: Champion Copper and Conqueror Oil (after pruning).

AUGUST Pip fruit: Champion Copper.
Stone fruit: Champion Copper with Mavrik.

SEPTEMBER Pip fruit: Fungus Fighter.
Stone fruit: Mavrik with Greenguard.
Roses: Bravo with orthene, alternate with Shield or Super Shield.
Tomatoes: Champion Copper.

OCTOBER Citrus: Champion Copper with orthene.
Pip fruit: Fungus Fighter (add maldison at petal fall).
Stone fruit: Bravo with Mavrik.
Roses: Bravo with orthene, alternate with Shield or Super Shield.
Tomatoes: Champion Copper.

NOVEMBER Citrus: Champion Copper with orthene.
Pip fruit: Fungus Fighter (add maldison at petal fall).
Stone fruit: Bravo with carbaryl (until harvest).
Roses: Bravo with orthene, alternate with Shield or Super Shield.
Tomatoes: Bravo or Tomato Spray.

DECEMBER Citrus: Champion Copper with orthene and Conqueror Oil.
Pip fruit: Fungus Fighter with carbaryl.
Stone fruit: Bravo with carbaryl (until harvest).
Roses: Bravo with orthene, alternate with Shield or Super Shield.
Tomatoes: Bravo or Tomato Spray.